THE
Open Heart
CLUB

GRIEF JOURNAL
*From Grieving to Living Again
After the Loss of a Child*

CHRISTINE MADRID VALENZUELA

The Open Heart Club
Grief Journal From Grieving to Living Again After the Loss of a Child
All Rights Reserved.
Copyright © 2022 Christine Madrid
v3.0

The opinions expressed in this manuscript are solely the opinions of the author and do not represent the opinions or thoughts of the publisher. The author has represented and warranted full ownership and/or legal right to publish all the materials in this book.

This book may not be reproduced, transmitted, or stored in whole or in part by any means, including graphic, electronic, or mechanical without the express written consent of the publisher except in the case of brief quotations embodied in critical articles and reviews.

Outskirts Press, Inc.
http://www.outskirtspress.com

ISBN: 978-1-9772-4492-5

Cover Photo © 2022 www.gettyimages.com. All rights reserved - used with permission.

Outskirts Press and the "OP" logo are trademarks belonging to Outskirts Press, Inc.

PRINTED IN THE UNITED STATES OF AMERICA

Dedication

To my powerful and loving tribe- my husband, Louie, my daughters Jana and Sofia, and my granddaughters Naya and Iliana, who have journeyed along with me and who have been a constant source of support, strength, and love. And to my sweet son, Louie, who continuously inspired and prompted me to share.

Table of Contents

Introduction i

The Hummingbird 1

Shock 9

Devastation and Denial 19

Anger and Frustration 31

Lost and Searching 43

Exploration 54

Connection and Signs 65

Insight and Landing 80

Introduction

I AM WRITING this grief journal and sharing my experience of losing a child because I have had a persistent feeling of obligation to share this with others. When I started writing this journal I didn't sense fulfillment but instead deliverance. As I completed each section about my son's death, I didn't realize all the restoration and rebuilding that was taking place in my own life. How could what I thought of as being such a horrible event in my life bring such a powerful and needed change? I would never have seen this possibility when I started out on this project, but now that I am done, I can see that writing it all down has brought me salvation.

It wasn't until three years after my son, Louie, suddenly collapsed and died from an undiagnosed enlarged heart, at the young age of thirty-seven, that I decided I had to share my experience; because I felt compelled to do so. Every time I heard about a parent losing a child, I was filled with a sorrowful connection to that parent. Whenever I shared my struggle with another grieving parent, they were thankful to be able to share their gutting heartbreak. In many cases, we shared similar difficulties dealing with this new and painful detachment we felt and confusion about what death actually means. Did our relationships really need to end? Did we need to accept the finality of death in order to live full lives?

This was just too impossible to fathom. Acceptance was the biggest struggle of all. We talked about how badly we wished they were back in our lives; we shared the same strong wish for a connection to the love that we thought we lost. It became more than a desire for me, it became a goal.

Writing this book was tough because I had to relive all the initial feelings. It took a lot of self-imposed force to get myself to sit down and begin writing. What helped push me along was the ever-growing empathy I began to feel for other parents who had experienced the loss of a child. My feeling was that if I honestly expressed my story, it might help them express theirs. I know now that if I wouldn't have pulled up all the pain and sorrow, I would still be in a very dark and lonely place.

When I first began writing, I thought I was trying to find acceptance but I knew I needed more than this. I had one persistent question in my mind that blocked any kind of peaceful acceptance. **How can I restore my connection with my child again when I am still alive and he is not?** This was a mission that pretty much consumed me.

As I plunged deeper and deeper into my search for reconnection, another issue gradually surfaced. I began to consider the possibility that there may be a lesson I was supposed to be learning through all this pain. More and more I began to feel that it must be a colossal life lesson that I needed to investigate, and that this experience had to have a purpose. I reasoned that something that had such an impact on me and others had to have a lesson or a reason. The last part was hard for me to accept because I felt it was the cruelest way to learn. How could such a tragic experience teach anything beneficial? I never viewed my loss as a punishment of some kind because it is something that I, along with millions of others, have had to experience. I know that tragic stories or events have lifted humanity and so if there is a purpose for loss and sadness in the world, then I had to examine my own loss. Could my loss possibly uplift and transform me?

Another reason I continued writing was because my son has been my constant companion through this all. Perhaps he sees a need for healing that goes beyond my own healing. I'm still searching for the full meaning of this experience but I think that writing this journal is part of my purpose, and I would never have done this if I hadn't have explored my own heart and soul.

In this journal I won't speak much about Louie's precious life before death; I do this with his daughter, my husband, my daughters and all the family and friends who loved him so much. There is not an hour that goes by that I still don't think of him. We still celebrate his birthday because that was the beginning of the gift he gave us, and I still have days when my tears flow because I miss him so much, and that's okay because that's my normal.

I'm opening up about my journey so that you will begin to open up and begin yours. The circumstances surrounding the death of your child or loved one and the special memories of the life you shared with him or her are meaningful and sacred to you. When you use this grief journal you can think about your own personal experience. My intention is that my expression of words may be a channel for you to allow the flow of your own words.

The focus of this journal is about learning to reconnect to your loved one and living life fully again. It's not about getting your old life back, because you will forever be changed by the experience. I had to begin a new life, but first I had to get back the desire to want to live again. This journal is not about burying a child and waiting to meet again in the afterlife; that was not my focus. It is about reconnecting now in whatever manner or form in which it may manifest itself. You get to figure out what that might look like for you. I will share what it has been for me with all its pain, all its truth, and all its transforming love.

Journaling allowed me to look at my thoughts and feelings that were just welling up inside me and creating a cavern of despair. When I let all my words out to live in the light, a new perspective about my loss and his death developed. I was often surprised and unwilling to believe some of the things I had written down, but in time, I realized that it was part of my healing. Looking at my loss allowed me to see how broken my heart and spirit were, and this spurred a desire to feel whole again.

My wish is for your unbearable wound to be cared for and healed, even though the imprint will always remain. I am proof that the wound can be healed and the scar that remains can take on a new meaning. It can be transformed. I now look at this deep emotional mark as a reminder of the immense capacity we have to love, and how we can endure the loss and even become capable of sharing and giving more love, once the healing begins. I look at my broken heart as a heart that has been fractured. Just as a muscle or a bone strengthens under pressure, I believe that a fractured heart may increase its ability to feel more deeply from the stress it has endured. What feels like a broken heart now can one day feel more like an opening, which allows for more love to flow out and more love to flow in.

I have no clinical training in therapy or psychology and I want you to know that I was in counseling for a year and a half after my son died. It was a source of help and guidance that I needed and I do recommend it. I am only a mother who wants to share what I experienced in the hope that you will not lock your loss away, along with your desire for living a full life again. I also hope that this journal will help you investigate a new bond or connection with your child or loved one that you would like to establish again in some form. When I examined death and loss, I gained other perspectives and insights about not just living my life again, but about how I wanted to rebuild my life. I was definitely changed from my experience and so I began examining many old beliefs and practices that were once a part of my life. Many remained but some did not fit anymore.

I realize that grief can be isolating but it doesn't have to be a solitary experience. I encourage counseling from a professional or personal source if the process becomes too difficult, and please remember that I am also a living example of someone who is able to feel joy again while still feeling sorrow.

After Louie died, a friend who had lost his teenage daughter said that we now belonged to a club that no one ever wanted to be a member of, and it was so true. Even though I did not want to be his co-member, I was surprised at how connected I felt to him. I knew what was in his heart and the compassion we felt for each other was so powerful and supportive. I feel the same way about you. I don't know who you are but I wrote this journal for you. I started as a member of what I thought was **The Broken Heart Club** and evolved into a member of what I call **The Open Heart Club**. We share the same heartache and feel a shared understanding of its impact on our lives.

I've shared some excerpts from my journal so that you can get a glimpse of some of my own struggles and gains. I hope it serves to help you with your own writing. What I have written may have an impact on you but what you write about your own story is what really matters. Allowing yourself to think and express your thoughts and feelings about this monumental time in your life may help you gain healing and insight about the person you lost and the person you can become. As you read this, know that my spirit stands with you, and I send you love and support. I hope that through writing your story you will be able to open your heart, lift your spirit, and eventually live a full life again.

Naya's drawing for her Daddy's card

The Hummingbird

THIS TINY BIRD has become a cherished creature to me and all the family. In this journal I've included the symbol of the hummingbird because it has been an important presence in my life since my son, Louie's, death. The image you see was painted by his daughter, Naya, after his death. We used the painting on the thank you cards that we sent out after his services. Before I explain why it has become such a symbol of connection and hope to us all, I'll first tell you about some of the symbolism and mythology regarding this incredible little bird.

There have been many ancient beliefs about this tiny bird throughout the ages. The indigenous people of the Americas have held many powerful roles for the hummingbird. The Aztecs considered it to be the soul-carrier that guides the departed into the afterlife. The Hopi believed that these small birds could bring back messages of guidance from the divine world during times of trouble. The Navajo considered the act of pollination as a life-giving gift and would celebrate the hummingbird with ceremonies of gratitude.

In modern times it is written that they represent strength and resilience, and the ability to experience **joy after great sorrow**. It is said that the central message of the hummingbird is that "**the sweetest nectar is within.**" Now for my story that began this project.

On the day that my son died, and before his body was taken away, I placed my hand on his heart and I asked him, no, I demanded of him, to send me a sign. I needed to know that my son was in a good place and that his spirit was at peace. No sooner did we walk outside his home and into his courtyard, when more than a dozen hummingbirds suddenly descended and lingered over us for at least half a minute. There was a larger red-crested one that lingered in the center, and then they all flew away. Family and friends who were gathered with us were just as surprised as we were. I went from the shock of having to say my final goodbye to my son, to suddenly finding myself standing in the midst of such a scene of beauty and hope. I was stunned with the possibility that maybe I could still communicate with my son, even after death. It felt like out of this shroud of darkness a sliver of light had pierced through, if only for a brief moment.

I took this as the first of many signs and messages that I would receive from my son. Soon after, I quickly researched the spiritual meaning of the hummingbird. What I learned, along with the symbolism of the small creature, was the first glimpse of a possible shift in grief, that I was not yet ready to accept. That sign my son sent me was full of hope and I sensed that he wanted me to view it as such. I took it as a personal message that I might get through this, and in time, understand more about his death and my life.

I couldn't deny that Louie was trying to tell me that he was in a good place, whatever that meant, but I was not yet ready to be at peace with this reassurance. I was just beginning this emotional and spiritual journey. I received the first of many signs on that day, which began my realization that there must be more I needed to explore if I was going to survive this. I clung to the symbol of the hummingbird and hoped that I too would again see the goodness in life, despite this tragedy. I started my deep dive into this uncharted, sorrowful journey and illumination and transformation surfaced. It's hard to believe but I have shockingly found more happiness, joy, and gratitude in my life from experiencing this great loss. Nothing is taken for granted anymore and the gratitude I feel for people and experiences has given me a whole new perspective on my life. I have somehow come to see this heartbreaking experience as an incredible awakening that my son wanted me to receive. I see it as an incredible gift of love from him.

Recording my thoughts and feelings has not been easy but what I gained from going into my pain has been life-changing. I don't feel like I did this alone. I always felt my son's love pushing me forward. Now that I have finished, I know why this was so important for me to do. I will always keep anyone who has gone through this sorrow and who searches for understanding and healing in my prayers. Be brave even when it feels torturous, be gentle with yourself and allow yourself to feel everything in your heart, and be truthful in your journaling. You may be surprised to find that what you believed about a situation was only your perception of it at the time. You may eventually even develop a whole new perspective about people and experiences and their meaning in your life. All this is possible when you come through your grief and back into living fully again. Blessings to you on this journey.

Journaling

Journaling

Journaling

Journaling

Journaling

Shock

I START MY book with **SHOCK**. I don't have any journal entries here because I have written the entire memory. It's been several years since this surreal event happened but as I sit to write it all down, it becomes crystal clear in my mind and my body. I recall it all: the temperature of the summer day, the taste of tears running into my mouth, the deafening silence in my ears as I saw family arrive, and what felt like the paralysis of my cracking heart as it struggled to beat with normal regularity. It floods back so easily. Even though recording this is hard, I'm glad it's found a place on paper, because it would have been too much to keep in my mind and my heart.

Before the day that I lost my son, I had been calling and leaving messages for him to join us for dinner. I didn't get too concerned when he didn't respond because he often took long bike rides or frequently enjoyed long runs. He loved exercising because he said the endorphins he received helped with his anxiety and recurrent bouts of depression. He was a single dad and sole custodial parent of his beautiful daughter. Because we lived so close to each other, I had the joy of helping him raise our granddaughter. She was staying overnight with us so I knew he would have the opportunity to get in a good long bike ride or run and would have some relaxing down time. We had company over and so I let the unanswered requests for him to join us go, and I convinced myself that maybe he forgot his phone or was getting some uninterrupted sleep.

The next morning, I invited him over for breakfast but again there was no response. By lunchtime, after many more text messages and phone calls, the worry started to spill into my gut and flood my mind and I decided to drive to his apartment and see if everything was okay. As I was driving there, I fought to keep down the sense of dread that kept rising up in me. Because Louie dealt with anxiety and depression throughout most of his adult life, I saw him or spoke to him on a daily basis. During this time, he had been feeling more relaxed and peaceful than he had in several years. I was always able to sense when my children were struggling over a problem, even before I spoke with them, but during these recent months I was beginning to feel some comfort in seeing him so calm and content. But once again, the old alarm bells within began sounding and I tried to fight the sense of panic that was rising up.

When I got to his building, the first thing I did was check the parking structure for his truck. I saw it parked as usual in his stall. This filled me with even more apprehension. I headed straight for his apartment. I had an intuitive feeling in my gut that when I turned the key my world was going to be destroyed. I remember putting the key into the lock and hesitating for a few seconds. I turned the key and stopped midway, and then continued to slowly open the door.

I entered and walked apprehensively into a space that was so immaculate and orderly that it seemed impossible for anything to be wrong. As I quietly called his name and got no response, I moved slowly through the hall and what continued to be a flawlessly ordered setting, until I glimpsed my son lying on the floor. He looked as though he was peacefully sleeping where he had fallen, but I knew a peaceful fall was a contradiction. The second it took to reach down and touch him felt like an eternity and for that second I fought with my hand to stop, but I continued to reach out. I knew before I touched him that his spirit had left his body. His sweet face had no warmth to the touch. I couldn't believe what my eyes and my hands were telling me. The sudden and violent blow of reality came down and shattered me. I quickly put up an imaginary shield that rejected the knowledge of his death, and the denial was like my weapon to destroy what my eyes were seeing. But then the millisecond of denial disappeared and I felt my mind and my body crumble.

The best word to describe what came next is lamentation; it's the passionate expression of wailing, sobbing and moaning. I didn't know it was possible for that much expression of pain to come out of my body and so I felt like part of me had to step out because it was more pain than I could endure. I was so overwhelmed by the pain that I instantly rejected the reality of it and again and again I tried to work my mother's magic over him to bring him back to me.

I quickly began to caress his arms and face and back as I willed warmth and life from my body into his still body. How could my mother's hands not fix this situation? I gently blew my breath over my boy in an attempt to share my life force with him. And all the while, only seconds were passing and the rational part of my brain was trying to silence the message that my worst nightmare had happened.

When his neighbor Joe appeared, he tenderly tried to give me support and consolation. As part of my brain watched all this, it felt like I was watching a slow-speed, silent movie. When the paramedics and police arrived, reality began to sink in and I knew I had to call my husband. I don't remember how I spoke those unspeakable words to him. I don't remember.

Family and close friends began to arrive. I remember sitting in silence and feeling like I was in suspended animation. I couldn't judge the passing of time. Once my daughters and husband arrived, we walked together to join Louie for the last time before he would be taken away from us. We knelt around Louie and said our goodbyes and this is when I laid my hands upon his chest and I demanded him to send me a sign that would assure me that he was at peace and in a good space.

I didn't know how long I would have to wait for this order, but I urgently needed to receive whatever sign that may come through. Upon walking outside his home, within minutes, more than a dozen hummingbirds filled the space directly above all of us gathered on his patio, and one larger hummingbird lingered over us. At the time, I was just as surprised as everyone else but my husband and daughters acknowledged the event and said to me, "There is your sign." I didn't realize at the time that it would be the first of many signs that I would receive from him. These signs of my connection and my bond with my boy have been an important part of my healing. I cling to every sign as a glimmer of hope to help me accept his death, not as an end to my relationship with him, but as a manifestation of the power of love's eternal bond.

The days that followed were surreal. His autopsy revealed that he died from an enlarged heart. They couldn't explain it and so it was labeled idiopathic, which means it was a condition that arose spontaneously and the cause was unknown. The explanation really didn't matter; all that seemed important was how we would all go on after this terrible sadness.

Whether the death of a child or loved one comes in a hospital room or on a battlefield or on the streets or in the home, it doesn't matter. We may be by their side or have had someone pronounce the horrific words to us, but the initial knowledge still feels the same. It's like a sudden violent blow that stuns and then begins to slowly saturate us in the pain. I'm recounting this to you because I know you have your own memories of the initial shock you received at the death of your child or loved one and this must be the point where your old life stopped and a new one had to begin.

It was definitely a crossroad for me, and at the time, I stood lost and confused at the intersection. I could remain in shock and grief or I could figure out how to incorporate this misery into the life that I was still obliged to live. My decision to choose a path didn't come swiftly. I lingered, stationary and lost for days and weeks. I want you to know that I am no longer there but it wasn't easy to choose my direction or even want to move at all. Staying a little numb and emotionally paralyzed became a sanctuary of immobility. Remaining in that state meant that I didn't have to think about what I was going to do after my child's death. I thought that staying in indefinite shock could work for a while. I was wrong.

This option didn't last for very long because I also had a grieving granddaughter to raise, and two daughters and a husband who were also in the depths of grief and needed care. I decided to mask my unbearable grief with denial and pretense. I reasoned that if I performed all the normal things that I did before, then everyone would feel good again, and I would resume some control over my life. In actuality, I felt like I was drifting farther and farther away from them, because all I wanted to do was to tether myself to my son's spirit before I lost him completely. This was my fear and my obsession.

As I write all of this in hindsight, it sounds so fear-filled and irrational, but how can anyone have a clear and orderly mindset when it feels as if their world has been destroyed? Guilt and obligation were the grounding cables that kept me connected to my family but I was just barely holding on inside.

You may know exactly what I'm describing. When I wrote all of it down, I felt like I was reliving it; it is intense and powerful, but remember, you are only recalling the event. You are now in a space to describe it, release whatever you want to say about it, and then when you are ready, move on into what comes next.

Take the time now to reflect and write your own personal thoughts and memories that surrounded your loss. Let your feelings about it flow freely because there is no judgment about what the heart feels. The important thing is to express it. If you have buried your unexpressed sorrow and loss with your loved one, you may have also buried some of your true spirit. By unearthing it all, you can choose a new perspective about it that will allow it to exist as part of your life rather than a fearful, painful episode that needs to remain unspoken and keeps you from moving forward.

There are many ways to unearth this sorrow. I have drawn images, I've written lines of poetry, I've let solitary words pour out of me that described my feelings and thoughts. Write or illustrate your story however you choose. This is an expression of your emotions and there is never any judgment about what you feel. The important thing is just to allow your emotions to flow.

I always saw my son by my side when I journaled; imagine your loved one along this journey with you. I believe that they no longer have to deal with problems, fears or illnesses like us; they can be spirits of love and support. They can send their healing love to you to help you through this process. Think of them by your side, sending only unconditional love and the desire for you to be joyful again; after all, it is only what we would want for them.

Journaling

Journaling

Journaling

Journaling

Journaling

Devastation and Denial

I DIDN'T REALIZE how difficult this period was until I took forever to write this section. I did everything to stall and avoid feeling the desolation again, but I had to remember it in order to write about it. I forced myself to delve into it again, because I knew that if after four years I still had apprehension at experiencing the pain of my loss through writing, what about someone who is still emotionally paralyzed in their grief? I didn't want anyone to remain stuck in that kind of misery, so I sat and I wrote. I recalled my worst memories when it felt like my world had shattered.

Journal excerpt

Well, I got through his funeral. I remember hundreds of people filling the church but I can't remember one single face clearly. I remember arms embracing me with their condolences but I can't remember who they were. I clearly remember hugging my sweet granddaughter as she broke down when she could no longer be close to her Daddy's coffin. I also felt like the most inept person in her life because I couldn't soothe her pain. And now all the activity has stopped and I have to think about all this over and over again. My mind doesn't stop replaying this horrible movie. I just want to forget.

The shock of my son's death was indescribable and planning his service was surreal, but the period after the funeral was the darkest. There were no more agonizing tasks to complete, like arranging church services, deciding mortuary details, writing eulogies, or planning a reception for loved ones and friends. Reality began to force its way into my life which forced me to acknowledge the devastation I was feeling. I felt as if my life had crumbled right before my eyes and I had no past or present strengths or structure to use to continue living it. The constant loop that played in my head was, "How could this have happened; how do I continue my life after the death of my child, and how do I keep my connection to my son?" The last question was the primary focus of my anxiety. I continued to walk amongst the living but I felt like I was a million miles away, as I tried to tether myself to my son.

Journal excerpt

I cooked breakfast, I dropped my granddaughter off at school, I went to the market and when the cashier asked me how I was, I began crying beneath my sunglasses. I can fake all human interaction but I don't want any. I just want to crawl in a hole, but I can't. I'm a responsible person so I will continue to fake it but I don't know how long I can keep this up. Is the ruse on everyone else or on me?

When I sat quietly in my grief, it felt like I was in some other twin dimension where I knew everyone could see me but I was slowly vanishing in my own suffocating atmosphere of anguish and despair. I believed that if I kept myself functioning within their view, no one would notice how lost I felt. At the time I thought that this would be the way I would have to function for the rest of my life. It was an exhausting deception to hide my disintegrating self from everyone else. I was wrong about others not noticing the deception. It was an exhausting charade and I didn't know how much longer I could continue the pretense. Then as crazy as it sounds, denial arrived as my temporary savior. The moments of unawareness that I experienced after my son's death were ironically the most comforting. The few seconds in the morning, as I began to awaken, were the best part of the day, because my brain did not remember the shock of the previous days. I relished the seconds of feeling that the world was in order and a new day was dawning. Sadly, those few pleasant morning moments would quickly vanish and a deep despair would enter again.

Journal excerpt

God I hate waking up! Nothing has happened and nothing is real until I'm awake and then the nightmare begins. I wonder how many mornings I have left before the temporary amnesia wears off? It's crazy- I only get 2-3 seconds of normalcy and then the madness enters- I reject this reality! Insanity is so much more appealing. If I could lose all touch with reality then this would never have happened- Oh God, I'm really desperate.

My mind couldn't fathom the reality of losing a child and so I began looking for new temporary illogical solutions. I remember telling myself that if I pretended that my son was on some remote location on the earth, like the Himalayas or Antarctica, I could better cope with his absence- death was too permanent a concept for me to accept. These little deceptions only lasted for fleeting moments, but at least for those moments the unbearable truth didn't exist. I kept reality and agony at bay.

I can understand why people choose to remain in denial longer than they should. I look at it now as a needed tactic of escape until I could better cope with his death, if that was at all possible. The danger for me was to linger in this false security of delusion, where my pain was numbed. I wanted to keep pretending. I didn't have the desire to face the stark reality of his death. How was I going to move forward to heal myself if I couldn't even face the truth? At the time, feeling anything but horrible seemed impossible. Thank God for my family. One day, as I looked past my torment, I saw theirs. I began to notice the pain that they were all in. I was so lost in my own grief that I forgot that they were experiencing all the same pain I had been feeling. We were all hurting, especially my granddaughter, who had just lost her Daddy. My unawareness over not helping them with their sorrow, or even just showing them mine and being authentic and present for them brought me back to the realization that I somehow had to face the truth. Slowly my sense of guilt and responsibility to family and my love for them is what painstakingly shoved me back into trying to get a handle on my sorrow and my life.

Journal excerpt

Every so often, the curtain on my window in my confined room of misery blows to the side and I get a glimpse of my husband's, my daughters', and my granddaughter's pain. I can't look at their pain for too long because I'm not strong enough to help them right now- so along with my grief, I add my shame. My arms want to reach out to them and my legs want to stand in solid foundation to support them, like the woman in me used to do, but I can't find her right now. If they try to lean in on my brokenness, they will all fall. My masked strength will soon be discovered and then what will I do!? I'm so ashamed that I haven't even brought this up in counseling, and I feel like such a phony.

    I wasn't sure how to do this but at least I realized that I couldn't pretend anymore; there was too much at stake. I knew that I wasn't functioning very well and I knew that I had to keep moving forward in order to heal, but I still didn't know how.

    I continued therapy and finally had the epiphany that this was not going to get fixed quickly. Trying to rush out of grief was only causing more anxiety for me. Once I accepted that this was going to take work, I lost a little bit of my fear about feeling so badly. I began to focus less on the "**when**" this feeling of despair would be over and I focused more on the "**how**" to work through my feelings. I decided to just allow my feelings to surface. This felt scary because I didn't know how much I would feel or if I could shut it off. As a result of unlocking my sorrows, I could finally experience small periods of relief. Holding in all that emotion was exhausting and it only kept me deep in this world of sad seclusion. I was so focused on containing my grief that I didn't realize it put me dead center in this vacuum of sorrow. I had to let it surface and expose it to light. Maybe that would bring me out of the darkness too.

Journal excerpt

I had a meltdown today. Everything just came gushing out. Something was said to my granddaughter that took me back to an old experience with my son. This lioness of a mother came out and I shouted that I wouldn't tolerate it! I just couldn't hold any words back and a torrent of thoughts and declarations poured out. When I finished and sat weeping and exhausted, I realized that I was thinking about how I wanted to live my life and take a stand for what I believed in. I was actually thinking about the future. As I write this, I know this has to be a pivotal moment for me- I have shifted a bit from hopelessness to engagement back into life. Something has awakened in me- there is another glimmer that has made it through the darkness. Mijo, (my son) stay with me.

I think that hearing myself express all of this fear and confusion in therapy and reading my journal entries gave me a little compassion for myself. I could hear myself and I sounded pitiful and sad, and so I began to see that it was no way to continue to live my life. As I expressed the longing for my boy, I came to my realization that what I wanted most was to feel a connection to him. If I was going to figure out how to remain attached to my son's spirit, I had to pull myself out of this dark and desolate place.

Somehow through all my sadness, I knew that my son wanted me to be whole and happy again because I reasoned that this would be exactly what I would want for him and my other loved ones. The only thing that was going to heal my sadness was to feel his spirit again and have some sort of connection with him still, despite death.

Although this is not the way I was culturally taught to look at death, I knew that there were things happening around me that I couldn't explain, and these signs were moving me closer to connecting with my son again. The blackness that surrounded me began to change to grey, then I began to focus on my son's presence rather than his absence. That small glimmer of hope returned, and I knew that I needed that connection NOW! I asked my son for his help to get me through this.

With this new purpose, I began to feel some emotional movement out of this paralyzing grief, but I still didn't know how to engage in my new focus of reconnection. I needed to do more investigation of all that I was sensing and the messages and signs that I was receiving from him. This was the beginning of a shift from grief to hope. Despite this newfound glimmer of hope, I realized I still had feelings about his life and his death to release. I knew this process wasn't going to be easy; I also knew that losing my son would always be a sorrow I would carry but I had to learn how to carry it with me into a full and healthy life. I finally had a new focus and task that moved me from the trapped state of grief into the possibility of purpose.

Journal excerpt

My mask has shattered and I'm standing before my family broken and weak but at least I'm standing in truth. If I want to be the best model for Jana, Sofia, Naya and Iliana then I have to show them that their vulnerability is the key to living their truthful lives. I don't want them to think of their sadness as weakness. I don't want them to bury their feelings. I also want them to know that all of their qualities are perfect because I want them to love who they are in all their honesty. I have been a phony but now all I want to be is real. I think they see me differently and they may be a little nervous and relieved at the same time. I didn't give them enough credit for seeing through my façade. I'm relieved too. I'm going to do a transformational workshop that Jana wants us all to do. She says it has really helped her cope with Louie's death and other events in her life. Sofia and I will do it together. I don't know what awaits me but at least I feel movement and I'm not staying trapped in grief.

What I want to stress to you is that I didn't move out of despair without acknowledging my sorrow. Once I stopped trying to masquerade my pain, I was able to use my energy and thoughts for some constructive help. I continued to use therapy and journaling as a tool to expose my sorrow so that it would not stay locked up in my heart. I wanted my heart to be filled with joy again and not just sadness. The life I shared with my son was filled with wonderful memories but death had made me only focus on the loss. I wanted to remember his entire life that had wonderful events and accomplishments. By dredging up all that pain to the surface I stopped it from burying his life. Looking at all of that grief was hard, but trying to silence it and keep it pushed down was even harder. The pain is as deep as the love.

I know what apprehension you must be feeling to revisit this dark memory because I felt the same hesitation, but tenderly allow yourself to express it all. If you are looking back at this time, then remember that you are not living it anymore but just remembering it. If this is all still very fresh for you, then allow yourself to release your emotions about it when you're ready to do so.

Take time now to truthfully let your feelings or memories flow about this difficult experience you've had. There is no judgment about how you express feelings; they are what they are and they often times evolve into other feelings. I know that when I look back at things I've written, I can see a change of perspective about certain events. The events didn't change but what I feel or have learned about them has changed. The important thing is to feel safe and entitled to allow yourself to do this. As you do this, feel the love around you from all those who want you to feel peaceful and whole again.

Journaling

Journaling

Journaling

Journaling

Journaling

Anger and Frustration

AS MORE TIME passed, I began to leave some of the exhaustion of grief behind. Being in the state of depression and grief zaps all energy or desire to feel happy again. I had spent many hours and days when I had no energy to leave the dark solitude of sadness, but now a change was happening. I thought my new direction of remembering our happy and loving times would help me to focus on reconnecting with my son, but as I kept exploring my feelings, other emotions emerged. I wasn't sure if I wanted to investigate these new feelings arising but I sure as hell knew that I did not want to go back to desolation and despair.

Journal excerpt

Now what do I do and why do I even have to experience something like this!? I just want my son back- a do-over. How can you figure out the important things in life if time is taken away?! Mijo (my son), can you hear me? I'm so pissed that I have no more tries, no more opportunities, no more minutes or hours or days with you. I hate this! I'm only seeing my regrets right now and I don't know of a more brutal feeling than regret. I see wasted, precious moments with you before my eyes. I didn't know that I wouldn't have a lifetime with you! Our happiness together is hard to pull up because I can only see what can't change EVER AGAIN! I'm angry with myself for squandering our time together.

I went from feeling so weak in body and spirit and slowly entered into a new energy involving feelings of frustration and anger all directed at myself. I was angry that I didn't have my son with me anymore. I was angry that I didn't somehow stop this from happening. I was angry that my life and the lives of my family were being ripped apart. I was angry that my granddaughter would not have her Daddy in her life. I was angry about all the regrets I had for the things I didn't do for him. I was angry that I took all our precious moments of life together for granted. My frustration about not getting a second chance at anything and everything was unacceptable to me, but I had no say in the situation. I was probably most angry at the thought that I had fooled myself into ever believing that I had control over the life of someone I loved so much. Little did I know at the time that this would be one of the greatest lessons that would have the most effect on the way I viewed my past relationship with my son, and my future relationships with everyone else.

Journal excerpt

I'm so angry at my foolishness and my faith in believing the old tenets of life: reap what you sow, have faith that all will turn out well, your prayers will be answered, etc. Curiously, I don't feel angry at God. Have I factored him out altogether- then maybe that is anger- I can't even feel guilt about my sacrilegious statement. I could never accept that God was a punishing force because that characteristic always seemed too human for me. I expected less ego from the all-knowing God. I attended 12 years of Catholic school and I am not turning to my faith right now. I don't believe this was an act of God. Losing my son isn't a punishment because atheists also experience this horrible loss. This misery is non-denominational. It's an equal opportunity destroyer, I feel detachment from God. Maybe I'll feel differently one day but right now I don't have a place to lean on. I'm angry and frustrated with myself for time lost with my son. I guess anger is better than self-pity; at least it has a lot more energy. The glimmer appears then disappears. I think I realize I'm in a process! WOW- the brain is surviving! But I'm still PISSED!

I had spent 50 plus years building what I thought to be a strong foundation for life and I experienced it all crumble in a moment. I knew

I had to find a new footing to stand on so that I could try to make sense of this tragedy but it seemed like a monumental task, and all my beliefs and securities were gone. I was angry at life **AND** death. I didn't want to participate in either.

Journal excerpt

I followed all the damn rules! I planned my life around my kids. I didn't drink too much, smoke too much or party too much; I tried to be a good example to them- how stupid of me to think that this was my insurance for their happy life. What's the point? LIFE=we yearn to love and be loved, then we spend a lifetime learning how to love, and then the final task is to learn to accept the loss of love. It would be so much easier if I could just say it's God's plan. I'm much too controlling for that.

At the time I thought of life as some cruel, mysterious game that had specific rules, but then those rules could randomly change at any given time. I was angry at the absence of "guarantees" in life. I followed the rules and everything still went wrong. I could accept the fact that tragedies happened, and I never felt immune to them, but I was always hopeful that I would be skipped for such events. Intellectually, I knew that things could go wrong in life, just not in MY life. This viewpoint caused me shame because I sadly realized I had selective empathy and compassion. Even my guilt at feeling so selfish about my loss made me angry. I was in such confusion with all this new powerful, dark energy fueling me.

Journal excerpt

Who said I get to be exempt? Why should I be exempt? I guess I can show sympathy for someone else as long as I dodge the bullet. Well, I'm pissed that it happened. So do I chalk this up to one of the mysteries of life- well, we might as well be playing a stupid board game. Am I responsible to put us all back together, because I can't even put myself together? Is some profound lesson waiting for me- well I'm not ready to learn- I'm just angry.

My son did not die at the hands of another or struggle with a debilitating illness, he simply collapsed and died. The anger that I felt about his death couldn't be directed at anyone; not even God, and so my frustration grew. I lost him to a force I could never compete with or defeat. I knew I had to accept death whether I wanted to or not, and being defeated by this invincible foe made me helpless and angry. It wasn't a fair fight. I needed to lash out at something and so my anger flew out in all directions. As my anger generated a lot of energy it also consumed a lot of energy. I was like a tornado of anger that was losing strength. More than being angry at death, I was angry at having to accept it unconditionally.

Journal excerpt

My brain might explode! "The Game of Life"- what's the point? Who invented it anyways and why does it have to be played? I have read that we choose to enter life and we choose to live it in a particular way so that we can learn particular lessons. REALLY! We live, we die, we learned? Right now the only valuable thing that I can take out of life is that I experienced love. Ironically, the thing I value the most about life is the thing that is causing the most pain. Can love really be lost?

My anger slowly evaporated and I unknowingly began to rebuild my foundation on less infallible beliefs. I was in a state of investigation. I always thought that I was in control of all the events in my life and when things didn't play out the way I wanted them to, then I was upset. How wrong I was. Being angry at death and fighting it didn't make sense anymore. In truth, there never was a fight- it was simply an event. Death was not an enemy, just a state of being. There was no fault to be placed. The truth was that my battle was imaginary and exhausting and I knew it was keeping me from connecting to my son in some undiscovered form.

Journal excerpt

So who can I blame? What are the game rules!? I can't even muster up enough energy to blame God because I don't even know what He means in my life anymore. My anger is exhausting and I'm no less confused than I was before all this venting- I'm just tired of trying to find a reason for death. The only thing I know is that DEATH came and left with my son. It has happened and there's no reversing it.

Once I accepted that he had died and was gone from the world, the constant need arose in me to connect with my son, and there was nothing that could stop me from trying to figure this out. I began to convert my energy from anger towards a new intention, reunion. The obsession was to urgently figure out how to stay connected to my son and keep a relationship with him. My belief was that not even death could separate us. I know this sounds crazy but this goal was my focus and my rescue. All I knew was that I was forced to bury my child, but I refused to lose him.

Journal excerpt

What do I want? I want my son back. How? Any way I can have him. Okay, then I need to get started. I know his spirit is still there and I just need to have him back in any way possible. I don't know what happens for him now and I don't want to hang on to him and keep him from whatever he's doing- if that's even true. I know that love is the strongest bond we have and that will always keep us attached to one another. This is my only certainty right now.

Having this new purpose was what helped me escape from my anger. This goal actually pulled me back into my life. It became my deliverance. Although some may view this new focus as unorthodox and unnatural, this is what returned me to life and to my loved ones. Trying to connect with my son in the afterlife, whatever that was, shifted me from anger and moved me back into love.

Journal excerpt

I remember the scripture about love in Corinthians 13:4-8, "… It always protects, always trusts, always hopes, and always perseveres." I will protect my relationship with my son by keeping it alive when he isn't, I will always hope that this love will fill my heart with more love than pain, and I will persevere to create the connection I need with him.

The energy of anger is a powerful force so I thought if I can use it and harness it, maybe I can direct it towards my healing. This is what I gained from my anger. This is the direction I decided to move towards. If any of this relates with you then first try to state any emotions of anger or frustration that you may have felt after your child or loved one died. Your anger may be directed toward the circumstances around the death of your child or loved one, at yourself or others, or even maybe at your loved one. Stating all my feelings of anger, confusion and frustration helped me to release them. I gradually saw the energy in all the anger rather than only the pain. You may not feel these emotions anymore but if you've never expressed them then they dwell in your memory, your heart and your spirit. They may still surface for you-perhaps in a different way than they did for me. Although they are feelings from an event in the past, the emotions may live in the present. I often felt the anger come up but I directed it to some other issue or target that had nothing to do with the source of my anger. I didn't like the way this felt because I think I knew that deep down inside, it came from my unspoken pain.

To express feelings is to uncover what may have been ignored, but what can now possibly be set free and understood. My perspective about my child's death is in continual transformation, but allowing myself to feel it, express it and then understand it has helped me. It was often times scary for me to state some of this anger because my feelings revealed the truth at the time of how I felt about things in life that I always held sacred. I realize now that there was no harm in saying what I felt because that was my truth then but not necessarily now. I see that I'm allowed to change and transform myself.

When you write about your experience, know that you're not alone in this solitary act of expression; your child or loved one and all those who have ever loved you want you to heal your heart and spirit; their love is always with you.

Journaling

Journaling

Journaling

Journaling

Journaling

Lost and Searching

EVEN THOUGH "LOST and Searching" doesn't sound like I was evolving through my grief, I believe I really was. My feelings moved from anger and frustration and I found myself fueled by a more positive energy. Releasing all the heavy regret and remorse left me a little lighter to now explore more uncharted ground. This new shift helped me get back into some sort of constructive flow with my life. I wanted a connection to my son so I had to regroup in positivity and leave behind the sorrow- at least as much as possible. I didn't know what stage I was entering but I knew I was open to explore alternative paths. Hope unearthed itself again.

It's amazing what the mind is capable of handling through grief, all the while trying to function through the routine activities of life. I was still working a job, raising a child, and even trying to keep a marriage whole and loving. These in themselves are tasks that require lots of focus and dedication. I was amazed that I was still able to nominally manage my life, even while on most days, I was falling apart inside. Searching for my son's spirit became my newfound commitment and it helped to keep me focused and strengthened.

Journal excerpt

Okay, you died- but that means nothing to me. Your physical absence does not keep me from wanting to connect with you in some way. I know you are still here. I know you are good and in a happy and high frequency of energy. I think I've got to get my energy out of such a low, sad place in order to connect with you- so I'm only going to focus on my love for you- not how much I miss you or how much pain I feel. I'll focus on just sending you all the love in my heart! I've been listening more to intuitive speakers on YouTube and I've been reading more about the vibration created from our emotions. Sadness creates a lower vibration and happiness and love create high vibrations. If I am in constant sadness or pain then it will be harder to connect with you, so I will try to change my energy- this has to be helpful regardless of what my goal is so, that's what I'm going to do!

Even though I had no idea how I was going to begin this journey of reconnecting with my son, at least now I had a purpose that was motivated by love instead of anger. Initially, it was my fear of being disconnected from my son that began this expedition but now it was love that was the motivating force that would see me through it. Love seemed so much greater than fear. The love I had for my son was limitless and powerful. I knew it was more powerful than the fear I held in my heart about losing him. Fear now felt weak and limiting. I was constantly trying to push it away and focus on the strength and unlimited power of love.

I tried reading religious books about grief and consolation but I couldn't connect to the message I was receiving with my goal. The books didn't discuss reconnection, they discussed our feelings and releasing them to a higher power. I was raised with Christian beliefs about God, and reaping the rewards of heaven in the afterlife, but I no longer accepted them as the only way or the only truth. If religion is an area that gives you solace, then I wholeheartedly respect your choices. You will know best what supports and fortifies you. The fact is that at that time I was in a different place. I have since moved back to a more spiritual/universal connection with the belief in some sort of Creative Force, God, Love- I'm still unwrapping and exploring concepts.

Journal excerpt

I'm finally not asking why you had to die because it doesn't matter anymore— It has happened and now I need to make a connection with you. When I think about how much I love you, my misery is pushed aside. I wonder what you are doing now. I somehow feel that you're trying to help me. I'm going to try hard to keep myself in a more positive space so that I can feel your presence.

Lots of new possibilities about the things that no one has ever been certain of, like death, the afterlife or the process of crossing over, began to cross my path. I questioned life's purpose and the role that tragedies and traumas play in it. I didn't blame God or a higher power for all this misery. I always believed that we are created from a source of infinite love. To be punished by such a loving source did not make sense to me. Pure love is unconditional and so to hand out such misery for the sake of punishing was just too much of a human quality for me.

Journal entry

I think about you wherever you are now- heaven, the afterlife, the other life; I don't know. You must be in the presence of absolute love. When you sent me the sign of the flock of hummingbirds I knew you were happy. That thought softens my sorrow- I have only always wanted you to be happy with or without me. I'm in uncharted waters now but I'm determined to unite with you in this other realm. I want to feel our connection again. Perhaps after I get this connection or as time passes, this need will evolve into something else, but for now, I think I will find peace in our connection.

I was open to many beliefs and closed to none. I didn't know what the truth was nor do I know what it is now. All I knew was that as time went on, I began to get messages from others and from signs around me that led to my belief that there is more out there than we know about or completely understand. When it came to reuniting with my son, I would close no doors.

As I began to take on all these new ideas, I felt Louie's spirit encourage me. I cannot explain to you in any rational way how this happened; I can only tell you that I was certain of it. I began connecting to my son's spirit and strangely I felt there was some purpose to all this. I still wanted him alive in the flesh but I would take him in whichever form I could. It felt like I shifted from lost and aimless to purposeful confusion. A tiny glimmer of hope once again began to peek through my state of upheaval and grief and this time it didn't leave.

Journal excerpt

I was feeling a little desperate this morning; almost panicky and I needed to make some sort of physical contact with Louie. I told him that I was going to walk around my bedroom with my eyes closed and I asked him to bump into me or tap my shoulder so that I could feel his presence. I know this sounds crazy but I don't care!

After doing this for a while I went back to bed feeling hopeless, ridiculous and crazy. I lay down and I rested my hands on my heart, one on top of the other and closed my tear-filled eyes. I told him that I just needed to feel him again. As my eyes were closed, I slowly felt the warmth and presence of his large hand materialize between my own hands. I did it! We did it!! I got him back for a few moments. I didn't want to open my eyes because I was afraid I would lose him. Slowly I felt the sensation of his hand leaving and my hands touching again. All I felt was love and gratitude. This is the second reassurance that I received, which secured my belief now that I didn't lose my son forever, and I actually felt sheer joy and contentment again in those brief seconds!

This new purpose to figure out how to keep our spirits connected, in any form, was my drive, and it gave me the focus I needed in this foreign world. It was scary to leave the intense and weirdly familiar envelope of grief. It cocooned me from living my life and people respected it; to a certain extent I felt they subconsciously feared it and so they kept a welcomed distance, which made detachment easier for me. Grief held me tightly and I also clung to it, but if separating from this dark, hopeless companion meant connecting with my son, then I would gladly detach myself from it.

I think I clung to my grief because it was a way of hanging on to my son. His death was the last emotional experience I had with him and so it was my last and most powerful connection to him. To let go of that would be to lose my last bonding moment with my child. I was wrong.

I had pushed all the beauty of our loving relationship as mother and child, and the first miraculous moment we became bonded to each other, temporarily aside, and I let the last moment take center stage. All of his thirty-seven years of precious life that came before that instantaneous moment of death seemed to disappear and I was only absorbed in his last moments of life. I could not let the end erase the beginning and the middle of all that life and love. I had to focus on the beauty of his life rather than what I thought was the tragedy of it.

Journal excerpt

I want to remember all the wonderful and funny and precious moments in Louie's life before his death, but the last intense moments I had with him, and the finality I felt, have been the most indelible in my mind. Death is darkening all the life that came before. I don't want this to happen- I now have to cling to his life. His birth was a powerful event in my life but I have to work hard to keep all the living he did throughout his vibrant life alive in my memory. I can't let death overshadow all of that.

This was a monumental transition for me; I actually began to move toward the light, which is where I knew his free and glorious spirit lived. Even though I carried the pain of losing my child, this was the point where I began to feel all the love that was the essence of our bond. It wasn't his death that kept me bound to him; it was the love we shared that was more powerful, even over death. Searching the possibilities felt so much more positive and promising.

Was there a point where you found a dim light at the end of your dark tunnel? Were you wishing for or also searching for connection? Was there something that helped draw you out of despair and helped lift your heart back into a lighter place? Can you recall all the love that you shared with your child or loved one? Writing about all the loving times you shared helps bring some joy back into your memory. You can tap into the love and not just drown in the loss.

Take time to write your thoughts, memories or emotions about those times and remember what a powerful force love can be. Investigate what may help or has helped guide you out of the darkness. Let your words flow and feel a small or at least temporary shift into light. You can survive this.

Journaling

Journaling

Journaling

Journaling

Journaling

Exploration

MOVING INTO THE different stages of my grief just seemed to blend from one state to another. As time went by, I would often wake up and just feel a little lighter. I went from waking with reluctance to just waking up. Grief had been a heavy, constant companion but now I realized room was opening up for another companion, hopefulness. I wanted more special experiences like the appearance of the hummingbirds and the holding of my son's hand. Connection was my goal.

Leaving behind this lonely state of loss allowed me to see the glimmer of a brighter horizon. Focusing only on my pain made me forget that there were plenty of others who knew what I felt. I was finally open to seek them out. I hoped that more healing was possible in that space. I just wanted to be in the presence of others who didn't need an explanation about my sorrow. I just wanted to share it and know that it would be understood. If there is anything I had learned in life about emotional upsets, it was that holding feelings in or burying them was never going to lead to healing. The time was right for me to try it. Perhaps they had their own stories of connections with their children or loved ones that I could listen to. It would be welcomed confirmation about this new realm that I was exploring.

Journal excerpt

I saw a friend in the market today. The first time I saw her here was just a few months after she had lost her son to cancer. We talked and she shared a few details about him and his illness, but I could see that she was still in shock, trying to process the unthinkable. My heart broke FOR her. Today I met her again but now I too have buried a son and now my heart broke WITH hers. It was as if now, when our eyes met, we felt arms reach out from our souls and embrace each other. We connected with love, compassion and an unspoken knowing. It was so sadly comforting to be held in her arms where words weren't necessary.

We shared our difficulties coping and we shared our reassurance of their presence in our lives through the signs we both frequently receive. We both share the hummingbird as our messenger from our sons' ever-present spirits. I know her pain and I want her to heal and I know she wants the same for me. It was such a comforting moment. I think I will look into a (bereavement) group.

I found a bereavement group in my neighborhood and I was soon invited to join. This setting was a new opportunity for me to open up and release some of the ceaseless supply of grief. The minute I entered the room that night I knew I was surrounded by loving and compassionate people. I was instantly connected to each one as they shared their sorrowful stories of loss. When sharing my loss with others who had experienced the same, I noticed that I was able to open up and be more vulnerable. We were able to reveal our wounds with each other with trust, and we listened and honored each other's stories.

But all the prayers, words and generous stories shared became difficult to carry. I couldn't sit in a room filled with so much pain and despair, and keep recounting and listening to heartbreak. The tool offered to help us heal was prayer. Trying to heal this agony with prayer only was not enough for me. If we were all asked what we wanted most it would be to have our loved ones back with us. I understood that this was impossible but I wanted and needed an alternative plan, which rejected the idea of the permanent separation of souls due to death. At the least, I wanted to discuss this desire, but it didn't seem like this thought would ever be explored. Although the phrase, "Let go, let God" had helped me in the past for other issues, it wasn't working for me in this situation. I returned to the group a few more times but I knew I wasn't on the same course as many of the others who were comforted with prayer. This was confirmed at my last session. I met a parent who joined us that night for the first time. (I have changed some of the details about this parent to respect their privacy). She sat hunched in her chair and her quiet sobbing was continuous throughout the night, in the small room. I was compelled to just reach over and pat her back every once in a while, to give her a bit of consolation and support. I even thought that perhaps her loss was much too recent for her to be able to participate in the group.

We sat listening as each person shared something about their loved one, and then it was her turn. She began to speak about her deceased son, a young nurse who left behind a beautiful wife and two small children. Between tears she spoke about how much she missed him and that she didn't know how she was going to go on without him. We all had empathy for what we assumed was her recent and traumatic tragedy. Then a woman asked her how recently her son had passed and she answered, "Twelve years ago." We were all shocked that this poor mother was living in such torment for twelve years. I was flooded with so many emotions at that moment. This poor mother's life ended with her son's death. I saw this pained soul, whose spirit was drowning in sorrow, and who now could only walk with the dead. She could no longer be a wife to her husband or a grandmother to her grandchildren. She was in the suspended animation of grief. Although I was entering a place of begrudging acceptance about my son's death, I saw the fearful possibility of burying my own spirit and not fully living life again. This mother's sorrow helped push me back into my life again. That night I decided that I didn't want to be like her and that I had to find a solution on my own that would work for me and keep me "alive" for my family.

Journal excerpt

Tonight scared the hell out of me! There was a parent in my bereavement group that is so stuck in grief and loss for the last dozen years that I could see how easy it would be to remain in this death-like state of misery and brokenness- this poor soul. I looked and saw the possible foreshadowing of myself- I know if I don't move forward, I risk burying my spirit. I have a family and I have a granddaughter to raise for my son. I have to figure this out.

For the first time I had urgency to find some alternative route or method to keep my bond alive with my child. I searched through books and writings about grief and healing. Some were generously given to me and others I sought out myself. I wasn't finding anything that I connected with or that addressed this unusual goal of making a connection with my son. I considered the flock of hummingbirds as my first message from him and then I received another message from him.

Weeks continued passing and I kept trudging through this grief with glimmers of hope and light. I did not like social parties very much because it was so exhausting putting on a happy face so as not to bring the entire celebration down. It's funny how synchronicity works. I decided to attend a family party and there I saw a close friend, who immediately pulled me aside. She said that Louie had come to her in a dream. I couldn't believe my ears. She recounted her dream to me and she told me that he wanted me to read a particular book; she even saw the title in her dream. She hadn't heard of the book herself but she told me that he was very insistent that she pass his message along to me. I was ecstatic that my son wanted to communicate with me but a small, comical, possessive, maternal part was a little disappointed that I didn't get the dream personally. I could almost hear my son laughing at this and shaking his head while telling me I'm crazy. It felt like a funny, normal interaction between the two of us. I felt so good; I got so excited and needless to say, my hope grew.

Journal excerpt

Wow!! I received a message from Brisia last night that she got from Louie in a dream!! He was insistent that she relay a message to me about a book that he wants me to read. I downloaded it last night and I'm almost through with it. It's the first book that I can relate to. It's about a mom who wanted to regain her connection to her son, and so she sought out a psychic/medium. I don't know if I'm ready to do this but I have such happiness and relief just to know that it has worked for her. It's like I got confirmation that I'm not alone in my quest and that he is there, like I've always felt. I didn't lose my son!

I couldn't get home fast enough to begin reading the book, *My Son and the Afterlife: Conversations from the Other Side* by Elisa Medhus. This book, written by another mother, who shared my desire to restore the bond with her child, finally addressed my goal. And the way the knowledge came to me reinforced in me that there was so much I didn't know or understand about the connection of our spirits, whether in life or in the afterlife. Medhus wrote about the tangible signs and messages she received from her son once she became more accepting of alternative channels. One way she spoke of knowing he was around was when she got a tingle on her leg. Six years ago, I received my first tingle on my left shin and it has also become my sign from my boy.

When I began to notice the signs and messages, I began to receive more, and so did other family members and friends who were close to him. My despair finally left and I was beginning to feel the spark of life return. I could keep moving forward if I released despair. I had hopefulness now and that was a much better companion. I had lived without my optimism for too long and now I got it back. I actually started to feel energized again.

Journal excerpt

For the first time I feel like I've crossed a major threshold into the state of reassurance and promise that I will continue my bond with my boy. My spirit is lighter, my heart is lighter and my thoughts are lighter. I even feel like I see my family clearly again rather than through the fog of my sorrow. I am so hopeful that I will find a way to survive this and still have my son with me again.

How has hope changed your grief? Hope has transformed mine. The loss never goes away for me but I was finally beginning to feel reunited with my son again, and I could feel my own spirit rising from the emptiness. A heavy darkness was finally lifting for me. I don't know if this is now a part of your experience or if you are still searching for ways to satisfy whatever need you have to help you heal. My need was to feel security that my son is not gone and connecting with his spirit gives me that security.

Take time to write about any emotional shifts along this journey that you have had or wish to have. Stating what you desire is as important as going after it. It's the first step in clarifying what you want and need even if it may sound crazy to others. I didn't care how my needs were perceived by others, I just knew that my goal was clear- I needed my son back in my life in whatever form possible. As the heavy sadness slowly lifts what do you hope for? Write it all- your desires, your needs and your hopes. Give a non-judgmental space for your spirit to express whatever is in you. Feel the loving spirits that embrace you and also want you to be healed as you continue this work.

Journaling

Journaling

Journaling

Journaling

Journaling

Connection and Signs

AS MORE DAYS, weeks and months passed, I was able to look back and it really felt as if I was on a journey. I couldn't believe some of the emotionally dark places I had been in and more importantly, I couldn't believe I was able to transcend those places and move out into light. Where before I was lost and wandering in this wilderness of grief, it now felt like I was moving back into the world and into life again on this new uncharted course. The horrible nightmare of losing my child was a reality. In my past were shock, desolation and despair. Although I didn't feel whole and content yet, and I wasn't even sure if I ever would, I wasn't in the gloomy abyss of those dark days.

I could still remember everything that had come before and I could still feel the painful emotions of it all, but the difference was that stepping out of this nightmare was finally an option. I was at last standing on a different foundation that was feeling more solid, safe and truthful. My old belief system about life and death had changed and continues to be in transformation. Things that I thought were sacred or unchangeable had shifted. New ideas were replacing old ones, and I must add that they are still today.

The realization hit me that if I'm on a journey then there must be some path that I'm following. I have no idea what I will encounter along the way or if I will ever reach a destination. Perhaps more will be answered for me when I finish this grief journal or it could be at the end of my own life. I have no answers and I don't really need a timeline for any. I just know that this is my course for right now- that much is clear. The other unexplainable certainty was that I knew that Louie wanted me to write about all of this and share it with others. I must admit that I have always had a curiosity for other theories or sciences that study time or dimensions, as do my girls, Jana and Sofia.

Because of our shared interest and because of our openness to explore other beliefs and theories about the metaphysical world, Jana invited us to attend The Conscious Life Expo in Los Angeles for the first time, eight years ago. It's an expo that covers a range of topics such as paranormal practices, healthy nutritional lifestyles, and UFO encounters! It's always been interesting and novel. We have now made it a regular event in our lives.

Some of the experiences there involved receiving messages from loved ones and after Louie died, we even received comforting moments of reassurance that Louie was close and that things were as they were supposed to be. I was told on a few occasions that he was at peace and in a very good place; this always gave me comfort.

Two years ago, I attended the expo with my daughter Jana. Jana and I had decided to go hear a speaker at the last minute, since we had spent most of our time eating our favorite Indian food, shopping and just talking with all sorts of people. The speaker we decided to go see was only chosen because it would fill up time before the actual presentation we had planned to see. We had never heard of him and weren't really sure about his focus.

We found seats in the front of the small room and as he began his presentation he told us that he was The London Medium, and that he would channel messages to people in the audience from their loved ones who have passed on. I was a little nervous because up to this point I had never asked for my son to come to me through a medium. If I ever received messages, they were spontaneous from people. I had spoken to him directly in my thoughts but for some unexplainable reason I wanted him to give me direct messages of his own. I suppose I didn't want to rush what I wasn't supposed to receive or what I possibly wasn't ready to handle. I definitely wanted to but something held me back. I gave Louie the lead on this because I felt that he was now in a place of more knowledge as opposed to my place of trying to grasp what was possible. My desolation about losing Louie had subsided with time, because it was undeniable to me that Louie was present and that we were connected again. Along with accepting my son's death, I also accepted the assurance that messages or guidance would come to me at the right time. My compulsive and obsessive need to constantly be reassured of his existence and connection to me had finally calmed down. I slowly gained some patience to allow things to happen in their due time.

Journal excerpt

Today we went to the Conscious Life Expo and Louie spoke to us through a medium! The medium came straight to me and Jana! (I didn't know that Jana was pointing to me so that the medium would be drawn over ☺) He had already spoken to several people with messages and information from their loved ones and all of those persons present were touched deeply by his information.

He walked toward me and said that a young man wanted to address us. He said the man was laying huge bouquets of flowers in front of us and he also said that I'd remember a time when he gave me flowers and he was in a bit of trouble. I laughed because he was talking about a time when he was nineteen and got caught drinking by the police. But then the amazing thing was that he made the face and the mannerisms that Louie would make since he was a small boy and wanted to get out of trouble! This fifty-something-year-old man turned sideways with his hands at his side and flashed the same devilish, charming grin that Louie would make.

He also told me that the "young man" was so happy that I was writing (the medium didn't say the word writing but instead mimicked writing by moving his hand, as if he were holding a pen, and then asked me if this made sense to me). He said that the young man wanted me to continue. He asked me if I knew what was meant by that and I said I did. Then he said that Louie wanted us to know how much he loved us and that he wanted the medium to tell us that he was holding us in a loving embrace. At that point the man became teary-eyed and said the energy was too strong for him and that he needed to walk away. The medium then said that Louie knew we would be there that Sunday to hear this, even though we didn't have any inkling about it. The medium laughed and said he didn't know either. My heart could not be filled with more happiness or gratitude. I love you, my son!

This seems like the time when the word **acceptance** entered my belief. I couldn't change my situation but I could begin to change my perspective on my new relationship with my son. I never lost the feelings of sadness and longing for Louie, but now they weren't the overpowering feelings of desperation that they were before. My focus now was working on creating some recognizable form of a relationship, because I was constantly being given messages that he was present. My grief was coupled with an eagerness to see what our relationship would look like. Now there were new possibilities surfacing around me.

Luckily one of our very close friends, Debbie Griggs, is a photo psychic. My girls and I met her seven years ago at the Expo and hit it off. Debbie and Jana became close friends and so she has been close to our family ever since. We often had her read our tarot cards for interest and fun. I trusted her as a friend and she had proven herself strong in her psychic abilities. She got to know Louie before he died and was close to us after he died. There were things that she would share with us about how Louie was doing in his new existence that I chose to believe and that gave me some peace. The information opened my mind about this new frontier both my son and I were in. She shared that in the afterlife, or as I like to think about it now, the other life, judgment and hurt were gone for Louie. He was strong in his spirit and wanted us to let go of any regrets, because he said that none of those things mattered. He wanted us to let go of fear and live our lives as we were meant to live.

The afterlife sounded complete and peaceful, not much different than my previous idea of a heaven. Thinking about my son in a positive environment gave me peace. A gateway to my son and a new reality was forming. Eventually, she told me that his energy was at such a high frequency now that it was difficult for him to try to connect with the low frequencies like mine when I was feeling sad emotions. When she said this, I decided to try to only feel love when I thought of him instead of sorrow. She said that love had a high vibration frequency and that his spirit was also in the state of love.

This was the key I was searching for from the beginning to help me regain my bond to my son. My greatest fear about losing him was diminishing and my hope to connect spiritually with him was becoming more real. Although I am certain that it is so important to feel all the pain and sadness of the experience, it was critical to not get stuck there. I finally reached a point where my life was no longer driven by grief but instead by love.

The messages and signs were always there but I had to move through my grief first before I could recognize them. Grief cannot be rushed. I moved along my timeline at my own pace and I know that others must do the same. I didn't see the signs around me until I was ready. Trudging through the experience of losing my son was important for me to recount so that I could work out so many misconceptions, thoughts and emotions. Eventually I gained more clarity and acceptance about his death. I realized that the only thing that matters in life is love. Learning to receive more love and learning to give more love was my lesson and my son has been my teacher. It wasn't until I was able to grasp this idea that I realized we were never separated at all. The love that bound our spirits from the beginning is eternal. Ah…I finally felt like I could relax and breathe. My **PANIC** was gone. My **OBSESSION** was gone. My **FEAR** was gone. I was welcoming **ACCEPTANCE**.

The signs that Louie sent us happened soon after his death. We all began to receive them. There were phone calls, lights flashing, songs, photos, dreams and lots of hummingbirds that he sent to his loved ones. All the family shared these strange yet heartwarming occurrences with the rest of the family as soon as they happened. Since then there have been many more signs, but I will recount a few that have been captured in photos.

One of the first signs we received after Louie died was from inside of his apartment. My niece Vanessa felt called to take a photo of one of his bedrooms where he liked to work out and read. It showed a dim violet light in the center of the room. In my conversations with Debbie, she explained that a violet light is one that has a high energy frequency and that it looked like Louie was coming into his new higher frequency.

A few months later, three Halloween photos displayed a brilliant violet light in them. Vanessa and my sister-in-law Maria took a photo together and a brilliant violet light appeared across their faces. When they noticed it, my sister-in-law posed, as if she was with Louie by her side, and when they looked at the photo, the violet light was right next to her. A close friend, Marc, who was present, saw it and with delight said he wanted a photo with Louie too, so he posed with his arm around my invisible son, and when they saw the photo, the violet light was standing tall directly inside of Marc's embrace. Within those same early months, his aunt Maria received a Facetime call from my son's cell phone, which at the time was in my possession in a cabinet without battery charge. She took a screenshot of this incredible call.

The last sign I'll share, although there have been countless others, happened three weeks after he died. My granddaughter, who loved to draw rainbows, called for me to come upstairs to her bedroom; she said I had to see something. When I entered her room, there was a full circle rainbow, from ceiling to floor, shining around her bed where she was lying down reading. I tried to figure out how this was happening. There was a small metallic homework tabletop that was by the window in the opposite corner of her room but only a small inch of it caught the sunlight and it had been there for weeks. This was the first time a huge rainbow had manifested in her room, much less circling her entire bed! Her words were, "Look what my Daddy sent me." She had no doubt it was a sign of love from her Daddy. I took a photo of this message of love because I knew I couldn't explain it.

We all continue to receive signs from Louie, and when I share my stories with others, they too have their own stories to share. A friend who had lost his teenage daughter had a memorial gathering for her at his home, and he said a white butterfly arrived at the beginning of the gathering and didn't leave until the end. It lingered for several hours and landed on many family members and friends. He said he knew it was the spirit of his daughter and it brought everyone great joy.

Because of all we have been taught, I know that some of this is difficult to believe or accept, but I have no doubt that spirits or souls that are connected by love can never be separated. Connecting with my son on the spiritual level has resurrected me. Some may say these signs are coincidences but I don't believe that and neither do others who have had similar experiences.

I know that the death of a loved one has been the hardest experience we have ever lived through and we cannot reverse the event, but we can transform it. It's not having that person in our life anymore that is so hard to accept. Realizing that my son's spirit is always accessible to me lightened my loss. It makes my reality more tolerable and if that is all I can have right now, then it is better than nothing. The "nothing" was not acceptable to me. If this is how you feel, then I hope my words have been of some help and comfort.

I don't know where you are on this road toward healing but when you feel ready, write your feelings about the possibility of receiving signs or about the actual signs you may have already received. If you feel that the connection is possible then express your thoughts and hopes. If you're not sure then you can also write your thoughts and emotions about that. There is no right or wrong for your process. It is yours and you will know what feels true for you. This is hard work but know how much love surrounds you through this process. You're not alone in this work. Love surrounds you and holds you close through the process. Know that your loved one is present and guiding you through your journey.

Journaling

Journaling

Journaling

Journaling

Journaling

Vanessa and Maria with "Louie"

Maria with "Louie"

Marc with "Louie"

Naya's Rainbow

Insight and Landing

IT HAS BEEN six years since my son died and four years since I began writing this journal. The process hasn't been easy and I have walked away from this work many times. As the months passed, I kept returning to what felt like the "scene of the crime." I had to look into the dying and wounded spirit that was once my own. It was like performing surgery on myself, which doesn't sound like a good idea, but I was the only one who knew how to investigate the wound and administer to its healing.

I feel like I've had a few reincarnations on this journey because the person who began this pilgrimage does not feel like the same one who is coming through it- and I say this because I continue to have insights about his death. I experienced lots of fear at letting go of old stories that were never really true for me, but I clung to them as my foundation. After my life got blown up with the loss of my child, I could have done two things: I could have retreated into my dying spirit until we both disappeared, or I could have made the choice to resurrect my spirit and return to living fully again. For a time, I did do the former and it was a welcome and needed escape, but all the love around me slowly pulled me back to my reality and fueled my desire to heal myself from this event in my life.

Today as I look back on my process, I'm much kinder to myself now for the mistakes I've made. I could only work with what I had at the time and it wasn't much. I am now so much clearer about the direction of my life. I wake up and try to do the best, using love as my compass. A broken heart can bring the gifts of vulnerability, compassion, and the knowledge that LOVE is really what matters. I still work hard at trying to live my life from a more loving center and I still often fall short, but now I'm aware when I'm off course. For me that is huge.

My mother gave me an incredible life lesson when I was young but at the time it was beyond my comprehension. I see how profound it was for her to know this. She had lost a daughter, Julia, after six months of life. She never spoke about it because it was too painful and she sealed the story in her heart. When I was thirteen years old I found out from an aunt. I was upset that my mom hadn't told me that I had a sister and I asked her why she hadn't shared that with us. Her words were, "because I buried her." I thought her words were peculiarly cold because my mother was a very gentle, warm woman. She then went on to say that, "God gives you his children to care for and love, but they really belong to him." Back then I thought my mom had learned to be detached about raising children, but what she and my father practiced in their own way was acceptance; the hardest lesson of all. I can see now that this is how we were raised. They nurtured and cared for us but always allowed us to find our own path. It was their love that made us all choose well and we were fortunate to surmount our troubles and find happiness. Today I realize that they may have understood parenting more than anyone I've ever met.

I fell madly in love with the three souls that I gave birth to and my love was possessive and fearful of ever losing them. Now my perspective has changed. I am still madly in love with them but I see them as three separate souls who came through me to live their own life and purpose. I understand better now when to stand back and let them live out their own paths. That lesson was an epiphany for me. This was something my parents learned through their own loss.

I realize now how many of my life choices originated from fear and worry. I now try to have an awareness of possibilities but not a fear of them. My son's death has ironically given me more understanding about my life. I have gratitude for all the spirit-filled gifts that he's given me, as much as I have gratitude for all the gifts of joy and love that he brought me during his physical life.

I don't know if you have reached this point of feeling like you have landed on a more solid footing yet. It took me six years to land. You will have your own timetable. If you have, then express what gifts or knowledge or new perspective that you have received. If you are not here yet, then perhaps you want to wait to fill this last portion in, or you can express what you would like to receive.

    I don't know if all of this has helped you but that was the focus, the intent and the desire of all my sharing. We are members of what I use to call **The Broken Heart Club** but I'd like to rename it **The Open Heart Club.** We have all been given an unwanted but powerful experience. I believe that from the power of it we can draw strength and awareness. Others can take from our healed spirits and strengthen their own. We can be a support to others in what we know can be a devastating experience. I hope the healing and transformation happen for you and that you can pass it on to others like us through your actions, deeds or words. I hope you use this work or any other method or practice that feels right for you so that you can live your life fully and help a fellow member of our group survive and eventually thrive.

    Losing my son has made me more aware of others' sufferings and so my capacity to feel for others has increased my awareness of how important it is for me to act with love. I can only think of one thing that, for me, seems to be the most important truth about our existence in this universe; it is that we are made from love and we are here to learn how to share that love. This was a constant thought in my mind throughout this entire process. This is why I wrote this. I have felt my son's support and guidance as I tried to share my loss and my insights. I hope that this journal has helped you to examine your own loss and transform from grief back into life. I have to say that there is more beauty in life for me now because nothing is taken for granted. Gratitude is also one of the major gifts I've received and it enriches all of my relationships and experiences. I know that I have to live the gift of the life that I was given more fully, and I look forward to my sweet reunion one day with my boy. From the depths of my heart I wish you healing, insight, peace and especially LOVE.

Journaling

Journaling

Journaling

Journaling

Journaling

Printed in the USA
CPSIA information can be obtained
at www.ICGtesting.com
JSHW070523260124
55963JS00008B/24

9 781977 244925